# THE ROTARY SWING

*Simplifying the understanding of the golf swing to make the game fun again!*

## *Chuck Quinton*

FIRST EDITION

# The Rotary Swing™
# Simplifying Your Golf Swing

# Chapter 1 - Introduction to the Rotary Swing™

Keep it simple. Three of the wisest words ever uttered, yet, how often do we truly heed this advice when thinking about the game of golf? The game of golf and more importantly, the golf swing, can become as complicated as we dare to make them, but this inevitably leads to a point of diminishing returns. At some point, the more you dissect and think about the golf swing, the more difficult it becomes to play at your best and improve. It is not necessarily because the information is incorrect, but simply because you lose the ability to freely swing the club without your mind being cluttered. In fact, for many golfers and countless golf instructors there is an inverse relationship. The more they learn about the mechanics of the golf swing the *worse* they score. Conversely, the opposite can also be true. The more refined your understanding of the swing becomes and the simpler your swing keys become, the more likely you will become a consistent and better player. The trick is in knowing what information you need to know and weeding out all that you don't – which is more than you think.

Everything you will learn about the Rotary Swing™ from this book is designed around the principle of building a conventional, effortlessly powerful golf swing while keeping it simple! Once you learn the straightforward fundamentals laid out in this book, your golf swing will resemble those of many of the professionals you see on TV. There are very few things to learn and they are simple tasks, but it will require that you "unlearn" and abandon many of the things you may have learned in the past. But trust me, when you hit your first effortless shot with your new Rotary Swing™, you'll be convinced just as thousands of golfers have been convinced and converted before you.

Ask yourself, do you want to spend years learning countless complex positions in the golf swing and try and manipulate the club into these positions or do you want to go out and hit the ball the best you ever have *today*? It's a simple question with a seemingly obvious answer, but you'd be surprised how many golfers waste countless years studying overly complex technique that has dozens of intricate variations in order to build a so-called mechanically "perfect" golf swing, which they don't need nor will they ever achieve. At the end of the day, having an alleged perfect swing really has nothing to do with scoring well and enjoying the game of golf. Almost all the modern swing theories focus on manipulating the club into positions with overuse of the arms and hands, which are far and away the most difficult parts of the body to control in the golf swing because they move the greatest distance and at the highest speed and they are controlled by the smallest muscles. It is very difficult for the average golfer to learn how to consistently perform these movements and maintain them without hours and hours of intensely focused and consistent practice.

The club is the only thing that actually makes contact with the ball, so logically it would make sense that the various positions of the club throughout the swing would form the basis of golf instruction. That is exactly what has happened in the modern era and that is exactly the reason why golfers continue to struggle with their games and why handicaps have remained the same for so many years. Focusing on the position of the club throughout the swing causes the golfer to artificially manipulate the club into those positions (usually by incorrectly using the hands) without learning how to engage and properly use the rest of the body– and it is these very hands that are the main culprit causing most bad shots by the average amateur golfer. The hands will destroy more golf swings than anything else as they can directly and dramatically manipulate the clubface throughout the entire swing with just the slightest twitch or twinge. Too much grip pressure in the left hand and the club won't release. Rotate them over too quickly and the ball hooks left. Try to hit hard with the hands and you can end up adding loft to the club and the ball goes shorter. The list can go on forever. No other body part can completely change the path and plane that the club travels on more quickly and easily than the hands. Because of the infinite number of problems the hands can cause, too much of modern golf instruction has been based on training the hands to work properly. Many of these instructors are the ones who tell you that you will get worse before you get better and that it will take years to master their theories. I will tell you that if I can't make you better in one lesson, you should find another instructor. I help golfers dramatically improve their ball striking by teaching them how to take these swing wreckers out of the picture and turn control of the club over to the more stable, powerful and easy to control big muscles of the body. But, perhaps there is a bigger secret to all this and that is that the club will actually automatically travel through the proper positions throughout the swing once your body learns the proper movements. Certainly, this will not happen without the use of the hands and arms, they definitely play their part, but I assure you they need not be the stars of the show. If the simple fundamentals laid forth in this book are performed correctly, the arms and hands can turn control of the club over to the body and take a free ride from the top of the swing into a solid and powerful impact.

Before we begin, do a little experiment with me. Take a golf club in your hands and extend it out in front of you like you were addressing a golf ball at waist height. Now, with just your hands, move the club all over the place as fast as you can. You should see that you can easily move the club erratically in any direction. Now, take your "address" position again and this time, try and move the club all over the place like you did before by just using your body, more specifically, your midsection or core, not your hands. You can still move the club, but not nearly as erratically or quickly as you can with the hands, right? Ok, so the hands can throw the club all over the place, so maybe you think the next logical place to look for control would be the arms, right? Wrong. While they are more stable than the hands, they still have a powerful capability to throw the club off plane and path and manipulate the clubface. That only leaves one thing – the body. The large, slower moving, relatively cumbersome muscles of the body are not only perfectly capable of controlling the arms, hands and club, but are also capable of generating a tremendous amount of power and speed with far less effort than the hands and arms. Realize that during a full swing with a driver, the club head effectively weighs as much as 100 pounds through impact and is traveling at 100+ mph. Relying on the small, twitchy muscles of the hands and arms is a great way to ensure you will struggle to reach your golfing potential and be very frustrated during the learning process, but you already know that or you wouldn't be reading yet another golf instruction book.

The simple fact of the matter is that the hands do play a vital role in the golf swing but it takes more practice and upkeep to maintain the feel and timing of how to use them properly. If you don't have hours to practice each day, you'll want to minimize your dependence on them as much as possible for squaring the clubface. As you will see in this book, it is the rotation of the body, and not the use of the hands, that will be responsible for squaring the clubface in your new Rotary Swing™.

So here's how it works in its simplest form: the hands swing the club, the arms swing the hands, the body swings the arms and the mind swings the body. Now if you reverse that list, you will get the order of importance of each part's role in the swing. This is what I call "the dog wagging the tail." If the tail's been wagging you for a while, this book will help end your struggles and you should see immediate improvements in your ball striking.

As you begin your journey into the "Rotary Swing™" you will begin to expand your golfing vocabulary with more productive words such as effortless, quiet, simple, compact, low-maintenance and powerful. You will also be in full control of your misses, likely for the first time in your golfing career. After reading this, you will be able to immediately identify, understand and correct misses in your golf swing. Most importantly, your swing will no longer be a mystery that suddenly deserts you on the 10th hole, leaving you wondering how you were hitting it so well just a few holes before. It will be simple to grasp and understand and your enjoyment of the game will improve dramatically. You will no longer find it necessary to "tinker" with your swing in an effort to find a swing thought for the day or some secret to the golf swing. This is the very same swing I teach to many of the professionals that I work with who play on the professional tours as well as amateurs and I can honestly say without hesitation that I have NEVER seen anyone not hit powerful, penetrating very high caliber golf shots when they follow the instructions contained in this book. In other words, if you follow what I outline in the following pages, you will hit incredible, effortless golf shots and be able to do so more consistently and will be able to stop worrying about your swing. However, this is not the greatest benefit of my teaching method. Sure, hitting spectacular golf shots is great, but you still have to make the putt, you still have to think your way around the golf course and you still have to maintain your body to be able to perform consistently day in and day out. But now that your swing maintenance is about to become dramatically simpler, you will have a lot more time to focus on these things and THAT is the greatest benefit to learning the Rotary Swing™.

# *Myth of the Perfect Swing*

The stacked compact position of the Rotary Swing at the top of the backswing.

In my mind, the greatest misconception about the skill of the professional golfer is that we all hit perfect golf shots every time. I can assure you, this is not the case. I maintain a plus handicap at my home golf club in Windermere, FL and I can show you my stats where I only hit on average just over 11 greens per round, and the PGA Tour professional will only average about 12 greens per round. This means the average professional golfer will have to get up and down to save par at least 6 times per round every time he or she tees it up. That means there are a lot of missed shots, bad decisions and bad swings in an 18 hole round of golf no matter the skill level. During my collegiate golf years, I felt that my swing had to be perfect for me to succeed as a professional golfer and that I had to hit perfect shots every time. My coach told me to work on my short game, I told him I wouldn't need a short game if I just hit every green like I thought I was capable of. I mean, why not? I hit several great shots per round in to the green, why can't I do it on every shot and every hole? After years of wasting time trying to "perfect" my swing and fit into some swing guru's theoretical model of the golf swing, I finally came to realize some invaluable truths about the game of golf and one of those was that there was no such thing as a perfect swing and nor would I want there to be.

The imperfections in the game of golf make it the beautiful and challenging game we love. If we all hit a perfect shot every time, the game would get pretty boring pretty quickly, it would be too easy and everyone would shoot 54 for 18 holes every day. The challenge of the game and the journey we take every time we tee it up is what makes the game rewarding and maintains our passion for the long term. You are challenged to dig deep within yourself to grind out a challenging 4 footer for par, to overcome your fears and doubts, to overcome your self. Golf is a game of self-discovery and challenge, for most amateurs, they will never come to understand and appreciate this most rewarding prize of the game because they are too busy trying to perfect their golf swings, mindlessly pounding hundreds of ball on the driving range. Trust me, it is a waste of time. Yes, you want to build and maintain a simple, solid and repeatable golf swing based on sound mechanics, but you must accept imperfect shots because you are guaranteed to hit them every day; they're as certain as death and taxes. My greatest hope in writing this book is that I can simplify your understanding of the full swing to the degree that you never worry about it again. From there, I'd like for you to explore the intricacies of the short game, course management, putting, hitting half shots, playing in the wind and the mental aspects of the game. I truly hope that you stop hitting "buckets of balls" on the range and start practicing hitting "golf shots" instead. I hope that you can accept your misses as a necessary part of the game and be confident that your new found time to practice your short game will get you up and down for par more often. I hope that you learn to enjoy the game again, as it was meant to be played and I hope that you stop bouncing from golf tip to golf tip looking for some secret to the game. The greatest secret to the full swing is that there is no secret, just sound fundamentals.

## *"Dynamicism"*

The last thing that I believe is important to mention before we dive into the technical aspects of the swing is the importance of swing dynamics. Part of the problem with much of golf instruction of the past is that it was taught in very static positions, seemingly putting off the motion of the swing and the dynamics involved until after the positions had been mastered. This type of teaching overemphasizes the position of the club and completely forgoes the flow of the swing and is obviously quite ineffective for the typical amateur given the average handicap has changed very little in the past 20 years. The golf swing is very much alive, a dynamic and athletic piece of poetry in motion in which the positions are secondary. Give me 50 different PGA Tour professionals and I will show you 50 different swings with the clubs in different positions throughout the golf swing. But the dynamics and motion of the swing glue all these positions together to form their swing DNA. So, how do you learn the dynamics of the golf swing? It's quite simple really.

If you were to grab your club and throw it down the fairway as far as possible, or, if you have ever felt the need to toss one out in the pond, or up in the trees, you would naturally create a very dynamic and powerful motion that, not surprisingly, would put your body, arms and club in the very same "positions" I describe in the drills in this book. The same is true if you were to take an axe and chop down a tree. You wouldn't think about the position of the axe, you would simply react to the task at hand and do most everything properly. This sense of the body being "alive" and dynamic is the exact same feeling you want when making a golf swing. It's amazing how many ailments of the golf swing go away when the golfer is mentally and physically "freed up" to swing the club naturally as they would anything else. Take casting the club for example.

From the top of the swing, many golfers will begin to throw the club toward the ball while the hands and the body remain static. Of course, you would never do this when swinging anything else, but a "dead" body will leave no choice but for the arms and hands to take over to try and get the club back down to the ball with speed. Have that same golfer throw their club down the fairway and voila', casting goes away. Never let your golf swing become a series of static positions. Think dynamic not static. A natural swing with good rotary swing fundamentals, forgetting about the arms and hands, will cure the cast and a multitude of other golfing sins.

The fundamentals I lay forth in this book are everything you ever need to know about the golf swing in order to develop a golf swing capable of shooting par or much better on a regular basis. We will keep it simple and focus solely on the fundamentals and you will be rewarded for your efforts. Now, let's get started.

# Chapter 2 - The Body - The "Engine" of the Swing

While I stated earlier that the mind was responsible for swinging the body, I will not start solely with a discussion of how the mind controls your muscles and affects the swing. It is too large and significant of a topic that would warrant an entire book, or even a series of books, in and of itself. Rather, I will weave important mental concepts and fundamentals into each topic as we progress so that it is viewed as integration of body and mind rather than a separate piece.

The Rotary Swing™ is divided into three building blocks, or fundamentals. Each piece builds upon the previous fundamental and makes the swing very easy to understand and learn. They are also learned in order of importance, with the most important being discussed first – Body Rotation.

## The Foundation – Understanding Proper Body Rotation

The importance of the body in the Rotary Swing™ simply can't be overstated; mastering this fundamental will take you as far as 90% of the way to developing your powerful and effortless rotary golf swing. Best of all, this 90% is the easiest part to learn, practice and master. To begin learning the correct movements of the swing, you will start standing erect with your hips and shoulders level to the ground. Standing tall, cross your arms across your chest while taking a comfortable stance roughly shoulder width apart and place a club across your chest at 90 degrees to your spine. Center your weight between the insteps of both your feet and feel very poised and balanced. With your hips centered between your feet and your spine vertical, rotate your upper torso around your spine while keeping your head and the base of your spine steady and your shoulders perpendicular to your spine. Imagine there is a stake driven through your spine into the ground and you are simply rotating your body around it while imagining that your belt buckle stays in place. As you begin to turn back, your hips will begin to get pulled back with you when the tension between the shoulders and hips become too great. You want to keep your hips relatively quiet but they should be allowed to turn to accommodate the rotation of the upper torso. As you are rotating back, you want to become aware of the tension or stretching you feel in your left oblique area and the left side of your stomach (for right handed golfers) as well as the lower back muscles on the right side of your body. This is part of your "core" and it is an area of the body that is usually not focused on during the backswing, so you will want to become aware of this and focus your attention on it for now. As you continue to rotate back and approach a 90 degree shoulder turn, the stretch in this area will become intense enough that you will realize that your body is trying to get your attention. This is your cue to begin rotating back to the left and unwinding your body for the downswing. Understand that if your shoulders do not reach 90 degrees during this exercise that is perfectly ok. Because you are doing this in slow motion, there is no momentum or "Dynamicism[1]" to carry your shoulders to a full turn, especially if you lack flexibility. Do not try and force your shoulders back any further as you will, in effect, be disconnecting your upper body from your powerful core and will not feel this healthy tension which is perfectly suited for triggering the transition to the downswing and generating power. If you

---

[1] The synergy of the different moving parts of the body.

struggle to feel this, it is ok. Focusing on this part of your body during your golf swing is a significant change in your sensory perception and is something that will become more apparent when we introduce spinal tilt in the second fundamental.

So, as we get our "cue" to begin unwinding, what you want to feel is a "bump" back to the left created by turning your core back to the left and settling your weight onto your left side. This bump is, in essence, a release of the stored up energy created during the backswing and is the trigger for starting the downswing. This "bump of the core" to the left gets everything moving in the proper sequence and allows you to start the downswing with virtually no conscious effort, making it a very dynamic and athletic motion. As the bump to the left is progressing, you will then be able to use both sides of your body to rotate your torso back to the left. This is an important piece to understand. If you feel that you continue to "pull" with the left side, you will not be able to effectively use both sides of your body to generate power in the swing, and since it is effortless power we are looking for, two sides working in sync are obviously better than one. Without getting too overly technical, continuing to pull and dominate with this left side will tend to cause the right shoulder to be pulled out over the top and cause you to wipe across the ball, hitting weak cuts with your divots pointing too far left of the target. To keep it simple think of it this way, you have two sides so use them both! But the bump must be allowed to trigger the downswing first, from there you simply wish to use both sides to "unwind" and rotate the torso back to the left with controlled speed. It is vital that your head not move forward when performing this "bump to the left", but stays back behind the ball throughout the swing until after impact. Note that this will create some slight leaning of your spine away from the target coming into the ball as your hips move forward and your head stays back.

You will want to practice performing this motion smoothly, it need not be an aggressive or an extremely quick unwinding motion, think smooth and swift more than anything else. Master this motion; it IS your golf swing from this day forward. It is incredibly simple and straightforward when done correctly, but full of effortless power, control and consistency.

### *Fundamental One – Body Rotation Drill*

| | |
|---|---|
|  | At address, make sure your spine is vertical and your weight is centered between your feet. You want a stance that feels athletic and balanced and provides you with a strong sense of stability. Your hips and shoulders should also be fairly level to the ground, although a very slight tilt of the spine away from your target is acceptable. |
|  | As you rotate back, stay centered between your two feet, allowing a slight amount of weight to move to the inside of your back foot. You should feel very centered and coiled as you reach the top of the swing, with your lower body providing stability. |

| | |
|---|---|
|  | **Tip**: If you struggle to keep your lower body under control, favor your left side at address and maintain more weight on the left side throughout the swing and while performing this drill. |
| | As you unwind everything back to the left, let momentum carry you fully onto your left side. Your shoulders should rotate fairly level to the ground, just as they did during the backswing. If you were to lay a shaft across your chest as you perform this drill, it should always remain parallel to the ground and perpendicular to your spine. |

## Most Common Tendencies

When practicing this drill, there are several things you can do that unnecessarily add inefficient movements to the swing. While I would not necessarily go so far as to call them flaws, they are simply unnecessary movements that complicate and create tendencies that you should be aware of as they increase the dependency on timing and hand-eye coordination in the swing.

# Weight Shift

For years, a dual pivot move, or a significant shift of the weight into the right side during the backswing and then back to the left during the downswing has been taught as a fundamental of the golf swing. It is not necessary in a rotary golf swing and in fact, unnecessarily complicates the movement. I'd rather see the weight stay quite centered throughout the swing with momentum carrying the golfer up onto the lead leg during the transition and into the follow-through. If anything, it is better for the average golfer to err on favoring the left side throughout the entire swing, particularly with the irons where a descending blow is required. With the longer clubs, allowing more weight to move onto the inside of the back foot is perfectly acceptable, but you should never allow your weight to stray to the outside of the rear foot.

If you do shift, understand that the more you shift away from the target, the more you must shift forward during the downswing. You will need to focus your efforts on timing this lateral move in order to be proficient at it and this requires more practice, more athleticism and better rhythm. If you make a shift into the right side and don't adequately get your weight back onto the left foot during the downswing you will end up hanging back and not be able to make solid contact consistently. If you shift toward the target too much, you won't be able to rotate properly and this is a fundamental piece of the swing that is necessary to square the clubface at impact on the proper path. To keep things simple, stay more centered and focus on rotation with good rhythm rather than shifting. A good mental image is to focus on keeping the base of your spine, or your belt buckle, fairly constant throughout your swing.

## Shoulder Tilt

It is important that as you are doing this drill, your shoulders rotate fairly level, or parallel to the ground. To check this, simply place a golf club across your chest perpendicular to your spine. As you rotate back, make sure that the shaft does not tilt, it should always remain parallel to the ground and perpendicular to your spine.

It is very common for a student to dip the shaft beneath parallel when rotating back to the ball when performing this drill. This is one error you do not want to make and is simple to avoid by checking yourself in a mirror. When your shoulders tilt like this, you won't be able to keep rotating powerfully through the shot and will be forced to throw your arms and hands at the ball. From here, the ball can be missed in both directions leading to a long day of "military golf" – left, right, left, right. You want to move your right shoulder powerfully through the ball, so check your shoulder rotation in a mirror.

## Head Sway

The most common tendency I see in golfers learning this drill is for their head to shift far too much to the right during the backswing and it happens almost imperceptibly for most. It is important that the head not shift away from the target more than an inch or so; rather it stays quite stationary as the body rotates around the spine. This shift is another extraneous and unnecessary movement that adds yet another element of timing to the swing. The head can rotate on the way back; it just shouldn't shift much away from, and definitely not toward the target during the backswing. If you've been letting your head move a great deal laterally during the backswing, keeping the head stationary will immediately make your swing feel more stable and under control. It may even feel like you are reverse pivoting when doing this, but fear not, this feeling is perfectly acceptable as long as it is not over done while performing the drill.

# Chapter 3 - The Second Fundamental, Forward Spine Tilt

If you've made it this far, you are halfway there to becoming a much better ball striker. I can not emphasize enough the importance of the previous body rotation drill, as this drill simply builds upon that foundation. In fact, everything about the Rotary Swing builds on the first fundamental and each piece discussed in the rest of this book simply builds on top of them sequentially and in order of importance.

The angle of the spine tilted over at address has received a lot of attention over the years and has created a great deal of confusion out there for the amateur golfer. When I teach a person how to address the ball, I use the terms athletic, balanced, ready and dynamic. If your posture and address position meets those criteria, you have little to worry about. However, I do have a simple drill to help you achieve a balanced and athletic posture at address with the proper amount of spinal tilt.

Standing erect, place your hands on your hips with your thumbs on the back of your belt and your fingers against your hip flexors at the front of your thighs. From here, tilt your hands forward and bend at the hips as if trying to pour water from the top of your head while keeping your back relaxed and straight. In doing this, you are pushing forward on the back of your belt while "pulling in" against your hip flexors. This causes you to tilt the upper body from the hips rather than slouch from the mid back while maintaining a "tall", athletic posture. Tilt comfortably over, to a point where the center seam on your shirtsleeve at your shoulder is in line with the edge of your toes. You can check this by hanging a shaft down from the center of your shoulder and checking to make sure it hangs out over your toes, not the balls of your feet. I liken this position to being very similar to that of a basketball player preparing to shoot a free throw as he dribbles the ball or a shortstop in baseball, prepared to move in any direction. You should feel athletic, balanced and dynamic and very much alive with your weight edging toward the balls of your feet.

From your address position, place your arms across your chest again and do the exact same rotation drill you did earlier while standing erect. It will feel different from the last drill, as your hips will be kept more in place and not rotate back quite as easy while you are tilted over. Because of this, you will more easily be able to feel the stretching of the abdominal muscles in the left side mentioned earlier. As you rotate back, make sure that your shoulders are rotating perpendicular to your spine without any tilting or dipping back and through. To check that you are rotating properly, place a shaft across your chest again and rotate to the top of your backswing. From here, have a friend place another shaft just beneath yours at the top of the swing on the same angle. This shaft should be at 90 degrees to your spine. As you unwind back to the left, ensure that the butt end of your club "rides" on top of this shaft all the way down into impact. This "guide" will help you feel the proper rotation of the body during the downswing. I call this drill the "Slide the Shaft" drill. It is likely if you've had much golf instruction in the past, you may feel as if you are "coming over the top" or that your right shoulder is working down to the ball and out over your toes. Both of these feelings are correct and indicate you are making the proper motion for an on plane swing.

The more lessons you've had in the past, the more odd this drill will feel. That is because in typical golf instruction today, the golfer is taught to hold the shoulders back and keep them from rotating as late into the downswing as possible in order to give the arms time to get back in front of the body. This tends to cause the right shoulder to dip coming into impact as the hips slide laterally toward the target. If you have practiced this move in the past, you will feel more like you are making the mistake of swinging over the top, but, the shaft doesn't lie and when you see it on video, it proves that for the first time, you've actually rotated your shoulders perpendicular to your spine and on plane. When done properly, you will also have the very unique sensation that your right shoulder is working down to the ball and that your body feels more "on top of the ball." This is a great powerful feeling and this sensation is exactly what you are looking for. If you've never felt like you "covered" the ball with your chest at impact, this drill will introduce you to this feeling and help you get a feeling for the first time what it feels like to really compress the golf ball by hitting more with your body.

**Tip!** When actually performing a full swing, your shoulders will not actually rotate exactly perpendicular to your spine. Because of the dynamics of the swing and the weight shift onto the left side the right shoulder will come in a little beneath the shoulder plane during the downswing. However, shortly after impact it will be on plane again as you can see from the sequence below. The feelings of the proper rotation are what you are seeking from the drill.

The best thought for how to rotate properly on the way down is to imagine that you were going to punch the ball with your right side with everything you had. Imagine loading up at the top of your backswing and then driving your body into the ball as if you were trying to punch the ball down into the ground with all your mass. When you do this for the first time, you will get an understanding of just how powerful your golf swing can become by using your body correctly.

As mentioned earlier, the "unwinding" portion of the downswing involves the "bump" of the core to the left with a smooth rotary motion of the body to the left driven by both sides of the body. Doing this rotation drill from the address position mimics 90% of the golf swing and when done correctly, you will see that most all the things you have worried about or struggled with in your swing are now a thing of the past. Your hips no longer slide excessively; they naturally clear out of the way without you thinking about them. Your spine angle now remains constant throughout your entire golf swing, which will greatly improve your consistency and the quality of your strike. You will notice that you no longer lose your balance and swing out of your shoes. You can now rotate effortlessly and in perfect balance which will provide you more effortless power than you've ever experienced. You can't practice these drills enough; they are the essence of the Rotary Swing™. Anytime your swing gets off, return to square one and practice these drills.

The first three steps of the Body Rotation Drill with a tilted spine can be seen here. First, address position is very centered between my feet. As I turn back, I remain fairly centered and turn around the base of my spine. As the downswing gets under way, I make certain to set my weight onto my left side while keeping my head in place. The last picture exaggerates the feeling of turning the right shoulder through the ball and over the toes of the left foot during the follow through.

From down the line, you can see how to properly achieve the tilted spine position. Note how my shoulders are out over the edge of my toes. As I rotate, I focus on rotating my shoulders at 90 degrees to my spine, back and through. A good visual is to think of replacing your left shoulder at the top of the backswing with your right during the downswing, or to think about rotating your right shoulder down "through the ball" and "over your left foot". The last picture exaggerates the feeling of driving the right side through the ball just after impact.

## Most Common Tendencies

There are several tendencies in ball flight that can be caused by not rotating correctly. The great thing is that the drill is very simple to practice and once you have it down, you will immediately be able to feel and understand why you missed a shot the way that you did.

## Misses to the Right

This very common miss can occur when the golfer tilts his shoulders early into the downswing. When this happens, the body gets "stuck" since the shoulders have tilted instead of turned and the club will come too much from the inside, starting the ball to the right of the target line. An overly aggressive hip and leg drive causing a slide is the most common culprit. If your ball is starting off to the right and your divots are pointing to the right of your target, work on the "Slide the Shaft" drill and your overall body rotation.

Note that blocking shots to the right is a very close cousin to the dreaded snap hook when the shoulders tilt during the downswing and the body gets "stuck". The snap hook generally occurs when the forearms rotate very aggressively through the impact area and is more common in better golfers. The more experienced golfer will sense the club coming too much from the inside with the clubface too open. In an effort to square the face at impact and save the shot, the golfer quickly rotates the clubface shut. If this is mistimed to the slightest degree, the ball quickly goes left as the clubface is too closed by the time it reaches impact.

## Misses to the Left

Shots that are pulled or start left of the target line are the most common "miss" in the Rotary Swing and can be caused by several different things. The two most common culprits are arms that work out in front of the body during the downswing and shoulders that rotate too flat. It is important that the shoulders rotate properly in the golf swing and if you find yourself pulling the ball, make certain that you work on the feeling of your right shoulder working down toward the ball during the downswing and work with the "Slide the Shaft" drill.

## Losing Your Spine Angle

In the Rotary Swing™, losing your spine angle can cause the ball to go in any direction and just about every bad shot in the book can happen as a result of this flaw. We've already touched on one of the causes of losing your spine angle in the previous section on missing shots to the left. When you don't rotate your right shoulder back down to the ball and rotate your shoulders too flat, you will, in fact, be "coming out of the shot" and, hence, losing your spine angle. Predominant misses will be left, but you can hit it thin, right and low from there as well. But there are a couple more common causes of losing your spine angle that are also prominent and equally disruptive to making a good swing and getting a good ball flight.

The most common cause I see is for a golfer to drive their lower bodies too hard toward the target during the downswing causing their spine angle to change. While the legs and hips are an excellent source of power in the swing and definitely contribute, they must not ever take over the downswing and leave the upper torso lagging too far behind. Their primary roll in the swing is to provide stability and support for the swiftly rotating upper torso, while still adding power and speed. If you've struggled with an overactive lower body, quieting the hips and legs will provide you with an instant feeling of stability and newfound control in your swing. For golfers who have been taught to make a large lateral shift off the ball during the backswing and aggressively drive with the legs on the way down, one of the keys to mastering the correct movement is the "One Legged Drill." (Discussed in detail in the Drills Section of this book) But for now, consider that you can favor your left side at address and keep 60-70% of your weight on the lead leg throughout your entire swing, particularly when hitting your irons. This will help ensure your upper body has a stable foundation to rotate authoritatively through impact. Once you gain control over your lower body motion, you can move back to having your weight more centered between your feet throughout your swing.

The second most common cause for losing the spine angle is one that, unfortunately, doesn't have a simple quick fix. It is a lack of flexibility and strength in the hip area. The lack of flexibility generally emanates from weak and tight hip flexors. These very powerful muscles are good for a lot of things, but in the golf swing of the average golfer, they usually do more harm than good because they become tighter as we age and become less active. It is very important that you work on your flexibility in this area by consulting with a flexibility expert. Don't fret because hip flexor strength and flexibility is something that almost anybody can improve if they are willing to work at it.

While the hip flexors tend to be strong and tight, the abductor muscles on the outside of the hip tend to be overly stretched and weak. This is a direct result of today's sedentary lifestyle that has us sitting in front of a computer, desk or TV for 8 hours a day or more. When you are sitting, these abductor muscles are elongated and the hip flexors are shortened. If you don't actively work to balance this, your golf game will noticeably suffer. It is critical to have a proper and consistent stretching routine to enjoy the game of golf at your peak for many years. If you suffer from very tight hip flexors as many do, it is best to seek out a qualified fitness trainer, physical therapist, yoga guru or martial arts instructor to help correct this condition.

# Chapter 4 – The Third Fundamental-Passive Arms

Many will find it interesting that it has taken me this long to get to the arms, and I'm still far off from talking about the actual club. There is an age-old debate in the golf instruction world between swings that rely on the arms for power and swings that rely on the body for power and this divergence has created a very deep rift between instructors of the differing philosophies. Countless heated debates have been sparked over this topic that end in pointless circular arguments that have segregated the instruction industry seemingly beyond repair. In truth, both sides are correct because both methodologies work within their respective set of fundamentals. The ultimate truth is that few in the golf instruction world want to let the cat out of the bag that there are numerous ways to "correctly" swing the club and hit excellent golf shots. Just one look at the practice tee during any professional golf tournament makes it abundantly clear even to the untrained eye.

No single set of fundamentals exists for the golf swing, as I mentioned, there are numerous valid models and then countless variations to each and every model. In the Rotary Swing™ I present to you here, I strongly prefer that the arms are kept very quiet throughout the entire swing. I like to think of them as "athletically passive" and not limp noodles. Like the lower body, they play a supporting role in helping the body move the club throughout the swing and they have some very important tasks, but they must not dominate your swing. The only time I focus more on what the hands and arms do in the golf swing rather than the body is when someone has a poor impact position or they are learning how to manipulate ball flight (i.e., hit draws, fades, low shots, etc.). For 98% of the golfers out there, over-use of your arms in the golf swing will not help you in any way and will cause you to struggle with consistency and here is why.

It is very easy for the arms to directly affect the club anytime during the swing. For the golfer who doesn't have a strong sense of the club throughout the swing and tries to over accelerate the club for power, the arms and hands cause more problems than they cure. For example, casting the club from the top is often a direct result of tension in the hands and an instinct to try and accelerate the club from the top as quickly as possible to produce more club head speed. As with far too many things in golf, what seems to make logical sense produces the exact opposite result. Instead of the desired result of more club head speed and power, the dreaded casting motion causes the club to decelerate at impact as all the stored energy in the swing is released too early in the downswing.

Controlling the clubface angle at impact is another area that can be very difficult for someone who isn't blessed with exceptional hand eye coordination and lots of time to practice. The angle of the clubface at impact can easily be thrown off by a slight overuse of the arms and hands and since the clubhead is moving upwards of 100 mph, this can send the ball miles off course, in any direction. At the end of the day, clubface angle at impact is of critical importance as it is the single most influential factor in ball flight. I cannot stress enough how being off by as little as 1 degree can make the difference between a hole in one and shot that lands in the water. Or, as Ben Hogan once commented, it's a "devilish" thing to try and control. Now it should be clear that trying to consistently control the impact factors that affect ball flight with the small muscles in the arms and hands is something that takes a great deal of coordination and a lot of time to practice to maintain the sense of feel. It can certainly be done, but if you'd rather start hitting the ball the best you ever have today, with the least amount of effort, instead of spending hours a day beating balls on the range, passive arms is for you.

So, if the arms do have something to do in the swing, what is it? The role of the arms is simply to follow the lead of the body from start to finish. When they do this, wonderful things mysteriously happen in the golf swing without you having to work to make them happen. Powerful, effortless, penetrating golf shots are the direct result of properly using the big muscles to power the golf swing and allowing the arms to go along for the ride in the Rotary Swing. Given their limited role, there is very little to discuss on the position of the arms throughout the swing because it is very easy to learn how to move them correctly.

The club, the hands and arms should all flow through positions, as they are lead by the body. Every single golfer will end up in slightly different positions throughout the swing based on a number of different influencing factors, from body build, to grip, to ball flight preference. These variances make little difference for the most part as long as your arms do not become disconnected from your upper chest too early in the downswing. A properly rotating body and constant spine angle will do all the work for the arms and no conscious effort to guide the arms, hands or club is needed. Let me emphasize, learning to let the body govern the swing greatly reduces your dependency on timing in your golf swing, especially as it pertains to the traditional release of the arms, hands and club at impact. Your release will happen naturally when you "reprogram" your mind to let the rotary motion of your body drive the swing. You will soon learn that playing golf with a Rotary Swing is much more of a mental exercise to trust your rotation rather than a physical challenge in swinging the club.

To fully understand how the arms work, go back to your erect athletic address position we practiced earlier. With a club in your left hand and your right hand hanging at your side, extend your left arm out in front of you until the club is parallel to the ground and the butt of the club is pointing roughly at your belt buckle. Ensure that your upper left arm is connected to your left pectoral muscle. This sense of connection will help your body to control the movement of the arm rather the movement of the arms controlling the body. From this position, rotate your torso as discussed earlier in the Body Rotation Drill. NOTHING CHANGES! Your body should rotate exactly the same as it did in the drills earlier and you should feel the same sensations. The only difference is that your left arm is extended in front of your body. As you rotate back, you will notice that the club is moving on a nice arc around your body and is being powered by nothing more than the rotation of your body. Once you rotate your shoulders back to 90 degrees, the club should still be pointing somewhat at your belt buckle and your left arm remains connected to your chest with the club still parallel to the ground. Obviously, the club and arms never swung up on plane with your shoulders, so to complete the drill, they must be allowed to do so. Return to the address position and this time as you are rotating your torso swing the left arm up and across your chest simultaneously. As you are doing this, imagine a watch on your left wrist rotating clockwise slightly such that you would be able to read the time at the top of the backswing. This slight rotation places the wrist joint in a position where the momentum and weight of the club can act as a lever on the joint, naturally setting the club. There need not be any conscious cocking of the wrists and little rotation of the left forearm. If they are relaxed and your "watch" is allowed to slightly rotate, everything will happen automatically. There should be no conscious lifting of the left arm. As a consequence of the position where your shoulders connect to your torso, the left arm will naturally swing up and end up in a position that is somewhat level with, or "on plane" with your shoulders.

Once you are in this "top of the swing" position, you will notice that your shoulders, your left arm and the club shaft are all level to the ground and on the same plane. With a good grip, the clubface will also be parallel to the ground. From here, bring your right arm up in place to support the weight of the club. Notice I said that the right arm should be brought in place to support the club, not to change the club's position. Day in and day out I see students performing this drill arrive at the perfect position at the top just using their left hand, and then they wreck it by "steepening" the shaft when they place their right hand on the club. That is the reason for performing this drill with the left arm only. As you will learn, when the shaft is made steeper by the right hand, this places the club in an "off-plane" position from which, most golfers will tend to swing the club "across the line" at the top. From that position, the club is too steep and will have to be "shallowed" out on the way down to avoid the dreaded "over the top" move. Next in the chain of events, the right forearm rotates in a clockwise fashion that tends to get the club in a "stuck" position behind the body. From here the club will come in to impact too far from the inside. When the right forearm faces the sky on the way down, it means the club is coming too much from the inside and you are in jeopardy of hitting a big nasty block or hitting a snap hook if you aggressively rotate the clubface shut in an effort to save the shot. To make a long and bad story short, bring your right hand on the club quietly and relaxed and don't let it change the position of the club. The right upper arm should be roughly in line with the side seam in your shirt. It should not be pulled back behind it nor should it stick out in front of the hip. It should be neutral and relaxed in a comfortable and athletic position.

Once you have mastered getting into the correct top of swing position and can comfortably arrive here consistently, tilt your spine downward toward the ball to simulate being at the top of your actual golf swing. Pay close attention to what this position feels like. It will likely feel more compact than what you are used to, but poised and powerful. Now, from this position, freely unwind everything back to the left while doing nothing with your arms. Again, nothing changes from the Slide the Shaft drill you were doing earlier. Your body does all the unwinding and your arms remain passive. In fact, you can simply forget about them. If you focus on rotating your body your arms will come down into impact in the exact same place every single time with no conscious effort or interference on your part. Your divots will be shallow and consistent as long as you remember this correct rotation or, your "ABT's" – that is, Always Be Turning. Your swing path is now ideal and what's best is you have not given a single thought to the position of the club, the arms or the hands. You have the freedom to rotate as aggressively as you like, although, I recommend you focus on simply unwinding smoothly from the top with good rhythm and tempo so you stay balanced. Because you are using your big muscles to power the swing, it should literally feel like you are putting in 50-60% of the effort that you normally do. If you feel like you are still working hard, it is because your arms are starting to outrace your body and your body rotation is slowing down. I cannot stress it enough, but you want to allow the rotation of your body to swing your arms through impact. The softer you keep your arms, the further you will hit the ball with less effort.

**From address to the top of the swing.**
The left arm must swing up on plane while your body
turns to get on plane with your shoulders. During this
time, your "watch" rotates so that it faces the sky, as the
club gets set behind you, putting everything parallel to the
ground at the top of the backswing.

## Putting the Swing Together

Once you have done this drill several times and gotten a
sense for the new top of the swing position, try and take it a
step further. Starting from the top position with your spine
tilted forward, bring your body down to your address
position. From there, quickly swing the club back up so that
you match the same position you just felt at the top when
getting there via the drill. Do this several times until you
can achieve this position from your actual address position.
Don't be overly concerned about the path of the club on the
way back. Focus on rotating your body and swinging
everything up into this ideal position. If you struggle to
remember what it felt like, stop and repeat the drill standing
erect so that you can remind yourself what the proper
position feels like at the top. Once you have done this
several times, begin swinging through impact like before,

freely rotating your body back to the left while doing
nothing with your arms.

## Tendencies of Incorrect Use of Arms and Hands

When it comes to tendencies that are caused by overusing
the arms and hands in the golf swing, there are simply far
too many to list. Overactive and incorrect use of the hands
can cause the golfer to hit just about every single ugly shot
in the book. It is good to recognize a few of the most
common tendencies to help you identify your misses but
you won't need to know much. As you become proficient
at the Rotary Swing™ you will know immediately when
you've tried to use the arms and hands because you will be
able to feel it-it will take far more effort to hit the ball solid.
Pound for pound, the small muscles simply can't supply the
power that the big muscles of the body can and you will
sense it dramatically after you have mastered the Body
Rotation drills and hit your first effortless and powerful
Rotary Swing™ golf shot.

## Hitting Fat

Hitting fat or when the club strikes the turf before the ball,
is almost always due to the arms releasing too early in the
swing and overtaking the torso rotation. This is caused by
two separate tendencies that can create the same result and
they are often done together. One tendency is for the arms
to start to "go" hard from the top of the swing. This is very
common for golfers who have a very strong "hit" urge and
struggle to keep their arms passive. This urge is directed
into the arms and hands and even if the body rotates
correctly the arms release too soon and you hit behind the
ball. The only way to avoid this is for the body to rotate
incorrectly and lose your spine angle as a compensation to
avoid hitting the ball fat. Unfortunately, this

"compensation" often results in another problem, hitting thin.

The other way to hit fat is for the body to stop rotating, or to "quit" on the shot. Remember my acronym: "ABT" – Always Be Turning. The body must never stop turning in the swing or the arms will have the opportunity and propensity to release early because the momentum carries them out in front of the body. Think of your golf swing as a bullwhip. Your body is the handle of the whip and the arms and club make up the rest of the whip. As long as the forward motion of the handle of the whip is maintained, the rest of the whip will remain lagging behind, storing its energy. As soon as the handle of the whip is abruptly stopped, all the energy of the rest of the whip is released and flung forward. In the golf swing, this can lead to the arms being flung out in front of the body too early and a fat shot will occur. It is important that you learn to trust that the slower more smooth feeling of the Rotary Swing will still produce the adequate amount of power necessary for the shot. This is more of a mental exercise than anything else, but the results of the effortless shots you hit will not lie. Your best shots will feel as if you did nothing more than "turn and turn" and did so at about half speed. The arms will properly release on their own in perfect timing as long as the body does its job and continues to rotate throughout the entire shot. Trust it!

## Hitting Thin

As mentioned in the Hitting Fat section, the arms releasing early can also cause thin shots. When this happens the body senses the club coming in too steeply and in an effort to save the shot, the spine angle is decreased or straightened up to keep from sticking the club into the turf. Working on passive arms and smooth body rotation will help the golfer maintain the spine angle throughout the shot and avoid this mistake.

One of the other common causes for thin shots is a lower body that is overly active. This can happen when a golfer has learned the habit of shifting their weight to their right side during the backswing. If they have a quick tempo, they have to aggressively drive their legs toward the target in order to get their weight back to the left side. This can cause a semi out of control downswing where the right hip gets thrust inward toward the target line and as a result, the spine angle changes. The cure for this is simple. You must learn to quiet the lower body. For those golfers who prefer visual imagery I tell them to imagine that the lower half of their body is like a big old oak tree. This helps them imagine a more stable lower body that is firmly grounded throughout the swing. For others, I suggest they start the swing with at least 65% of their weight on their left leg and KEEP it there throughout the entire swing. The "One Legged Drill" in the Drills Section is an excellent drill to help overcome this fault.

# Chapter 5 - The Grip, Setup and Ball Position

The grip has been discussed in infinite detail in all the golf publications over the years and every author has weighed in on his or her view. It doesn't take long to figure out that there are as many ways to hold the golf club as there are ways to swing it. However, there is an optimum way to hold the club so that you can produce a consistent and proper impact position that produces the proper, flat ball flight. The key to striking the ball properly and, in particular, the irons, is having the hands leading the clubhead through the hitting area thus creating the proper amount of forward shaft lean and a descending angle of attack at impact. Of all the best ball strikers' swings I have studied, I have found that the best ball strikers with the most penetrating ball flight and hit their irons the most consistently have somewhere between 8-12 degrees of forward shaft lean at impact. Contrast this with the typical amateur who has 0 degrees to even negative shaft lean at impact and it becomes very clear why the pros hit the ball much longer and on a more penetrating trajectory. Why am I discussing this in the grip section? Because a proper grip is necessary to ensure a square clubface when the hands are ahead of the ball at impact. You need a grip that is somewhat stronger than "neutral" to be able to get the club in this position without having to manipulate the club with your hands through impact. While I don't care for an overly strong grip, I do prefer a grip where the "V's" formed by the thumb and forefinger on each hand point toward the right ear or right shoulder when viewed from face on. This ensures that the clubface will be square at impact even though the hands are well ahead of the ball at impact and well forward of where they were at address.

**Figure 5-1 The Proper Grip**
Note in the photo above, the line formed by the thumb and forefinger on the left hand point at a spot between the right shoulder and right ear. When the right hand is brought into place, it simply matches the left hand by pointing the "V" at the same spot.

# Ball Position

A common question from new students is what is the optimum ball position for the Rotary Swing. Many instructors like to give a hard and fast exact answer that the ball must be played exactly here or there, but this can be a little misleading. All golfers will end up with the ball in slightly different positions in reference to where it is played in the stance and in relation to the hands at address. It all depends on the overall dynamics of your swing. The fundamentals of the Rotary Swing provide a solid, simple framework that allows for deviations for a golfer's natural tendencies and ball flight desires. It is quite flexible as long as the golfer understands the tendencies his or her deviations from the framework will cause. For instance, a golfer who does everything well in the swing but likes to have a lateral shift toward the target during the downswing will tend to play the ball more forward in their stance since they are shifting the bottom of their swing arc forward when they move their body toward the target. However, just because you have a fair amount of lateral movement does not necessarily mean that you will have to play the ball forward in your stance. A golfer with a very strong grip and a forward press at address who plays the ball forward will have to hold on to the release of the club through impact to keep from snap hooking it left. The golf swing should never be confined to a set of governing laws about positions; there are simply too many dynamic forces at work that are unique to the individual. The golf swing must be considered to be tendency driven and those tendencies and their ramifications must be understood. Having said that, because there need not be much lateral movement in the Rotary Swing™ and all other things considered neutral, I like to see the ball position somewhere near the inside of the left shoulder, or approximately in line with the logo on your shirt for most iron shots. With the driver, I prefer to see it positioned slightly forward of this, more towards the center or outer edge of the left shoulder, to encourage a shallower and slightly ascending angle of attack.

The left arm will be extended straight at impact so the inside of the left shoulder is naturally where the bottom of the swing arc will occur. Thus, placing the ball slightly behind this spot is an excellent starting point to ensure a downward strike. My biggest caution is for the golfer new to the Rotary Swing™ to not start with the ball too far forward in the stance, as this will require the golfer to make a lateral move toward the target in order to make solid contact. This is especially true when it comes to the driver, as the golfer will tend to wipe across the ball if they make a proper body rotation with too little lateral shift. Once again, a good guide for the driver is to place it off the center or outside of the left shoulder. Being told to place it off the instep of the left foot is horrible advice because everyone's stance width will vary a great deal, as will the important determining factors such as shoulder width and individual swing dynamics. The logo on the left side of the shirt, or left pectoral muscle is a much better starting point for measuring where the ball should be placed in your stance because its relationship to the bottom of your swing arc will never change.

## Address Position

Well into the book and I am just now talking about the details of the address position? That's strange isn't it? In most golf books, they begin starting out with something placid and static, the grip, ball position, address posture, etc. These are the same instructors who tend to teach the swing as a sequential grouping of positions that must be adhered to in order for you to hit good golf shots. Experience has taught me that this is not the best order to proceed. I'm far more interested in the overall dynamics and fluid motion of a golfer's swing than I am the static positions. Most golfers are shocked when I tell them that I rarely use video during my instruction, and never on the first lesson unless I'm working with one of my tour professionals. It is almost blasphemy in today's golf instruction world but my students' results don't lie. A good golf instructor should be able to see a golfer's swing and almost immediately see the major destructors in the student's swing and in truth, tell just as much by simply looking at the ball flight. He should then be able to quickly formulate a plan to modify those things and present them to a golfer in a way that allows the golfer to feel the proper sensations for the movement rather than pointing out a specific position. For golfers who I work with extensively, particularly my touring professional students, we do video tape frequently and get more specific into positions because we are trying to tighten up our misses as much as humanly possible, so we get a bit more concerned with certain things that can only be seen using high speed video. But if you don't make your living playing golf and don't spend at least 20-30 hours per week practicing, you need not be as concerned with what is going on behind you in your swing as you may have previously thought.

With that being said, I do believe video can play an important role in today's golf instruction for visual learners. These types of students need video so they can see what it is they are doing versus what they think they are doing. The danger in video is that many golfers get overly concerned with matching position for position of what they or their instructor consider to be the "model swing." This is not only unnecessary, but can be disastrous for many golfers who naturally have certain unorthodox moves in their swing that are still highly functional. In the end, understand that there are positions that are fundamental for the Rotary Swing™, but they need not be done to perfection. Come reasonably close and you will hit very serviceable golf shots.

Now, let's discuss the address position in slightly more detail. As I've mentioned, the address position needs to be alive and dynamic and almost always in motion until the club is pulled away. If you find yourself standing still over the ball for more than a second or two, you are thinking way too much. One of my favorite golfers of all time, Ben Hogan, always had something in motion, his feet settling in, his famous waggle, etc. but you never saw him sitting over the ball for long periods of time. He stepped up to the shot, settled in, and hit it. All his thinking was done behind the ball allowing his swing to be more of a reaction to the target.

Our look at the setup position will start with alignment, or, whether the golfer should stand square, open or closed. In general, I will start a golfer with a square to slightly closed stance in regards to his feet and the target line and we make adjustments for his tendencies and preferences from there. Because of the rotary nature of the swing, the most common "miss" is a slight pull to the left for a right-handed golfer. Because of this, perhaps half of my students will end up "settling in" to their new swing with a slightly closed stance with their feet but with their shoulders and hips square to slightly open at address. I actually prefer a setup that has the feet up to 10 degrees closed with the shoulders square to a few degrees open to the target line. Now to many of you, that may sound like golf instruction heresy to not teach a square setup but there is very sound reasoning behind it and many, many fine golfers have played this way including Ben Hogan, Sam Snead, Luke Donald, Mike Weir and dozens more. This setup puts the golfer in a much more powerful position and enhances their ability to rotate aggressively through the shot with better support from the left side while hitting more with the body.

It also makes it easier to hit more from the inside with a better sense of overall connectedness. Note that this applies mostly to all the longer clubs. As you get down to the short irons and wedges, the more upright nature of the swing with these shorter clubs lends itself to setting up more square. Now, let's talk about some of the details of this setup.

First off, one of the fundamentals of the Rotary Swing™ is that the arms are connected to the rotary motion of the torso. In order for them to feel connected and strike the ball more with the body, they must be somewhat "behind" the body coming into impact, which also means the shoulders must be somewhat open at impact. We achieve this powerful impact position by swinging the arms back behind the body during the backswing and start doing so in the very early stages of the backswing. However, when you set up with your shoulders slightly open of the target, this automatically "pre-sets" this connected feeling right from the address position and makes it much easier to make the golf swing feel compact. Because of the powerful rotation of the entire torso throughout the swing, it is vitally important to have a strong sense of stability in the lower half of the body. By setting the feet slightly closed at address, it provides an increased and enhanced sense of stability as you rotate into the left side in the downswing. While an open stance is not forbidden, it does predispose the golfer to having the right hip kick in toward the ball at impact, causing a loss of the spine angle making consistent solid contact difficult. Therefore, a square to somewhat closed stance with the feet is ideal.

So what about the arms at address? Well, this is another area where we can buck conventional golf wisdom. Because the shoulders can be square to slightly open at address, the right arm can actually sit somewhat higher than the left when viewed from down the line. Again, this is something that you can see in Ben Hogan and numerous other great ball strikers. Due to the rotary nature of the swing, you will naturally be coming more from the inside at impact, so it is not necessary to add to this by setting the right arm beneath the left at address. This is also a by product of something that can be seen in the golfer from the face on view. Because you don't set up with your spine angle significantly tilted away from the target at address for most shots, the shoulders will sit more level to the ground and this in and of itself puts the right forearm in a slightly raised position such that it will cover the left when viewed from down the line. This helps put the right side of the body in a more dominant position so that it can be used to provide power in the swing.

Once you have these setup positions down, the goal is to feel very athletic and balanced over the ball. You should NOT move your weight to your heels at address. You want your weight in the center of your feet moving more toward the balls of your feet. Observe the photo in figure 5-2. If you're used to setting up with your legs locked in place and your weight out toward your heels, you are going to feel much more athletic and poised when you have your weight properly balanced.

**Figure 5-2 – Address**

At address, note how a line drawn vertically from the edge of my right knee is out near the edge of my toes. This has my weight distributed evenly throughout my feet and places me in a very "ready" position where my body feels very alive at address. Also note that my feet are slightly closed to the target line while my shoulders are square.

From the face on view, it is vital that we get one thing correct – the position of the head. This has everything to do with ball position, so as long as the ball is in the correct place, the head should naturally setup in the correct place directly behind the ball. If you were to draw a vertical line straight up from the back of the ball, it should be even with or even slightly in front of the left side of the head as can be seen in figure 5-3.

**Figure 5-3 – Head Behind the Ball**

Whether hitting a driver off the deck or a short iron, it is imperative that your head start out and remain behind the ball throughout the entire swing.

# Chapter 6 -The Backswing

Once it's time to get the swing underway there are a lot of dynamics at work. Our first in depth look at the backswing begins with the takeaway. The takeaway is not just the club head moving back the first few feet off the ball but the motion of the arms, body and club working back together. The takeaway is one of THE most dynamic and underrated parts of the golf swing. Because golf starts from a semi-static position and because the ball is stationary, many golfers get very stiff and static when standing over the ball and their takeaway reflects this, setting the entire swing off on the wrong foot. Worse yet, is that most golfers are fixated on what the golf club does during the takeaway and totally ignore the body. Nothing could be more damaging to building a powerful and dynamic rotary golf swing.

During the takeaway, the things I focus on most in my students are how alive and dynamic it is. I want to see the body initiating much of the movement and the clubhead to move last or at least in complete synch with the body, but generally not first. All golfers start the swing somewhat differently, but the effortless body-driven golf swings start with a slight forward press of the club with a little lateral bump of the body toward the target. This is followed by a rebound shift back to the right to get the body rotating around the right leg and base of the spine. All of this is so slight that most golfers can't see it unless they are specifically looking for it or are studying it using slow motion video. But this subtle movement is what breathes life into each and every golf swing and is just as important as any other aspect of the swing because it keeps the golfer from snatching the club away with the hands and promotes a smooth rhythmical start to the swing. Of course, you can't think about all these things, so the key is to start out thinking about "flow." Set your swing in motion with good rhythm and flow and good things will follow.

Once the body has things moving in the proper sequence, we focus on where the club goes. I like to see the club either work back on the shaft plane established at address, or work back slightly beneath it. In all honesty, it's not going to make or break your swing either way and a quick glance at the practice tee at any PGA Tour event is testimony to this fact as you will see guys sweep it well to the inside (like Ray Floyd) and guys practically lift it straight up off the ground (like Jim Furyk). I am more interested in the club swinging back in synch with and working behind the body while developing a sense of connection with the rotating torso than I am the exact plane the clubhead travels back on. I use the plane the club is traveling on during the takeaway as a corrective measure when things go astray. I do not use club plane as a definitive path the club must follow. I'm more concerned that the club is on plane at the halfway back point, so if it's a little under or a little above the plane during the early stages of the backswing, there's not much to worry about.

That said, things can quickly go astray when the clubhead gets well inside the hands and under the plane early on. This is perhaps the most common fault I see in most golfers learning the Rotary Swing and it can cause some serious struggles. It is important that the clubhead not stray too far behind the hands when the club is parallel to the ground. Ideally, it should be inline with the hands, but once again, there is room for some variance here. I draw a box roughly around the golfer's hips as a guide to where the clubhead can safely be at this point in the swing as illustrated in figure 6-1. In most amateur golfers, the clubhead ends up well behind this box, indicating a swing that is too flat and a takeaway that is too "handsy." These golfers need to work on getting the clubhead to move back in the Safe

Zone and the swings will be consistently on plane and be much easier to repeat.

**Figure 6-1 – The Takeaway Safe Zone**
As long as your clubhead is somewhere in this box when the shaft is parallel to the ground, your takeaway is ok. Both of these takeaways fall within the box and they are both within the Safe Zone.

When the club reaches a point parallel to the ground, signifying the end of the takeaway, the angle of the clubface is another quick check you can make to ensure your swing isn't headed into troubled waters. For most golfers, I recommend that the clubface be square to the plane, or in a position that approximates your spine angle. Because we want to drive the swing more with the big muscles of the body and rely less on the hands to control the club, keeping the clubface slightly "looking at the ball" during the takeaway helps ensure this. To some, this may appear to be "closed" on the way back, but don't worry, it is perfectly ok.

A clubface that remains square to the shaft plane encourages a steeper plane during the takeaway. Because most amateurs tend to get the club moving too far behind them and swing too shallow often caused by the early rotation and rolling of the forearms and an early right wrist hinge, this helps mitigate this tendency. Secondly, it helps keep the hands quiet during the takeaway, which helps minimize manipulation with the twitchy hand and arm muscles. Remember, the hands remain quiet at this point in the swing with minimal forearm rotation and this will create the sensation that the clubface is looking at the ball longer during the takeaway.

**Figure 6-2 Takeaway Clubface Angle**
Note that during the takeaway the clubface appears to be "looking" at
the ball as opposed to rolling to a "toe up" position. This takeaway
works well with the shallower nature of the Rotary Swing. Note also
that while the clubhead has worked back slightly below the plane, it is
square to the shaft plane established at address.

## Halfway Back

Once you reach the halfway back point in the golf swing, there are several things to be checked. If we look from face on, we are looking for only minimal lateral movement, if any, of the head from where it was at address. A slight turn away from the target is perfectly acceptable but a large lateral move of more than an inch or two will make it very difficult for most golfers to get back to their left side during the downswing. If you are a golfer who struggles with getting everything back to the left side during the transition, you will be far better served keeping your weight more on your left side throughout the entire golf swing. In fact, I would suggest that unless you are a single digit handicap, that you focus a great deal of your time on becoming proficient at the "One Legged Drill" in the drills section of this book. This will teach you how to properly rotate your body back and through in the swing and dramatically simplify your number of moving parts. Even if you are a single digit handicap, this is a very viable way to swing the golf club and many great golfers have exemplified this type of "hanging on their left side" look in their golf swing. Jose Maria Olazabal is a good example of a golfer who makes a minimal shift into his right side during the backswing, particularly with his irons, and he is a phenomenal iron player. Some of the more modern players have also adopted a similar philosophy with regards to the weight remaining on the left side. These include Aaron Baddeley, Mike Weir, Dean Wilson and Will Mackenzie.

From down the line, we get a different and perhaps a better look "under the hood" of the golfer's swing and this is where we notice things can go bad in an otherwise good looking golf swing. There are two main checks that are of significant importance. First, when the swing reaches the 9 o'clock position, or when the left arm is parallel to the ground, the club should be pointing at the golf ball. Most amateurs err on the side of being too flat where the club points well outside the ball and this is a swing killer as it makes it very difficult to come down on the proper plane and make solid contact without a tricky manipulation of the club with the hands and arms.

The second key check at this point in the swing is that the hands cover the right bicep. You want the arms working more around the body to achieve the proper position at the top, so it is important that at this point in the swing they are behind the chest and over the right bicep. Both of these key factors can be seen in figure 6-3.

**Figure 6-3 - 9 O'clock Plane**
When the left arm reaches parallel to the ground, or 9 o'clock, the shaft should be pointing at the ball and the hands should be covering the right bicep.

## Top of the Swing

At the top of the swing, from down the line, we see the hallmark of the Rotary Swing. The arms and shoulders end up on the same plane at the top of the backswing. If everything up to this point is done mostly correct, this position will be achieved automatically. But why do we want to reach this position at the top? Why is it so different than what has been traditionally taught where the hands are high and above the right shoulder? The simple answer is that we want to use the body for power much more than the arms.

In most any golf swing, the better golfer will always end up in this position at some point in their swing. A golfer who swings their arms very upright like Jim Furyk or Sean O'hair eventually has to flatten out his swing during the transition to get the club on a plane where they can effectively deliver the clubhead to the ball from the inside. In the Rotary Swing, you achieve this position automatically and avoid the extra step of flattening the shaft at the top or in transition, which is very difficult for the average golfer to master without countless hours of practice. The end result is that your swing has fewer moving parts and, thus, is less dependent on the timing and athleticism that is required for this delicate move.

More importantly, this position is vital to the swing because we are going to be rotating everything, including the shoulders, through the impact area with great speed. If your hands are high above your shoulders at the top of your swing and have not adequately swung back behind you, you will end up coming "over the top" on the way down leading to a pulled golf shot. However, with the arms being much shallower at the top, the golfer has the ability to freely rotate everything during the downswing and "hit" with the body turn for a powerful strike.

**Figure 6-4 – Top of the Swing**

At the top of the swing, we are primarily concerned that the left arm and shoulders are on the same plane. Note the position of the right arm as well. It is not collapsed or pulled dramatically behind the body. The bicep on the right arm is inline with or just in front of the shirt seam on the right side of the body.

**Figure 6-5 – Face On**

From the face on view, you can see that there is minimal movement of the head from address to the top of the swing. In fact, it is perfectly acceptable to have even less. The key here is that the body has pivoted around the base of the spine. The hips and upper body have both rotated around a centralized point creating a very "centered" feeling to the swing.

# Chapter 7 - Downswing

During the downswing, you need to be primarily focused on a "bump" to the left by settling your weight over your left foot and turning the core to begin the body rotation. When the arms start to overtake or out race the body, the club can be thrown out over the plane resulting in a shot that starts left of the target. Therefore, it is imperative that your arms only play a supporting role in transporting the club down to the ball while the body rotates back to the left. There are some simple visual checks that can be made to help detect this in your golf swing in case you can't feel it happening.

In figure 7-1, you can see that the club is automatically carried down on to the exact same plane it was taken back on during the backswing when the arms do nothing but simply go along for the ride from the top of the swing. The body has rotated a great deal already, led by the core which is already square to the target line at this point and a "bump" to get the weight settled onto the left foot. When the club is in this position, all systems are "go" for the body to continue rotating powerfully through the shot.

## Figure 7-1 – Downswing 9 O'Clock

The arms are carried down into this position if they remain soft. The rotation of the torso back to the left with the soft arms allows the club to come back down perfectly on plane. Note how close the left arm is to the body still this late into the downswing demonstrating a swift rotation of the body with very quiet arms.

As the body continues to rotate, carrying the club down into impact, there is one other crucial check that can be seen from down the line. To ensure that you are attacking the ball from the inside, it is important that the club travel on plane such that it appears to go right through the right forearm as shown in figure 7-2. If your shaft appears above the forearm, this will inevitably lead to pulled shots. If it is too far under the right forearm, this indicates you are approaching the ball too far from the inside and the ball will tend to start to right of the target line. Just remember, "through the middle of the forearm for the middle of the fairway."

**Figure 7-2 – Shaft through the Forearm**
As the club is coming down, we want to make sure it is traveling through the right forearm to approach the ball from the inside of the target line and on plane. This very desirable position is achieved naturally when the body rotates properly and the arms and hands are left quiet.

## Impact

When the arms are kept passive, the club ends up on plane throughout the downswing, making solid impact automatic and a foregone conclusion. It makes your golf swing simple to keep in check and easy to self-check when your swing does get a little off. At impact, you can see that my shaft is on plane and the shaft and my right forearm form a straight line. Your main goal through impact is to keep rotating your body to the left and keep your arms soft. The softer you keep your arms, the further and more consistent you will strike the ball.

**Figure 7-3 – Impact**

At impact, the right forearm and shaft form a straight line and are on the same 9 o'clock plane the club was taken back and through on. The shoulders are slightly open to the target line and the hips are well open and continuing to turn. From face on you can see the hands leading the clubhead through impact and the head remaining behind the ball.

While the downswing is really little more than rotating or unwinding your body back to the left, many golfers struggle with understanding what the proper impact position should feel like. The most important key to a proper impact position is that your hands lead the clubhead through impact as show in figure 7-3. In other words, your hands must be ahead of the ball before the clubhead makes contact. As a result of this the shaft is leaning toward the target at impact-as many as 12 or more degrees in very good iron players. This forward shaft lean is one of the reasons the pros hit their irons so far and is one of the most common mistakes amateurs make in their golf swings. Most amateurs release or cast the clubhead very early in the downswing and the clubhead ends up overtaking the hands before impact. This makes it nearly impossible to control trajectory and very difficult to control direction because of the timing necessary to strike the ball with a consistently square face when the hands are flipping through impact.

So, how do we get this forward shaft lean? It's important that your body continues to rotate through impact while your arms trail behind your body. As long as your hands don't actively flick the clubhead at the ball, they will be "dragged" through impact by the rotation of the body. In doing this, it is also critical that you keep your head behind the ball at impact. If you slide your body laterally during the downswing rather than rotate, it is possible your head will be pulled in front of the ball when you reach impact. When this happens the club will be coming into impact open and too much from the inside and your misses will be blocks to the right unless you flip the clubface square with your hands. If your hands are active through impact and you flip the club with your hands you can hit hooks, blocks and the occasional straight shot. The difficulty is timing this flip consistently to hit the ball straight and it's not something you want to try and do, so it is best that you make sure you keep your head behind the ball until it is pulled around in the follow through.

# Chapter 8 - Swing Sequence Discussion

## Frame 1 – Address position

In figures 8-1, note the red line I've drawn up from the ball through my right elbow. This plane line represents where my shaft will be when my left arm is parallel to the ground, or the "9 O'Clock" plane as discussed earlier. Note that it is not the same as the shaft plane at address because of my more tilted over spine angle that is fundamental of a Rotary Swinger. You can also note that my feet are somewhat closed to my target line but my shoulders and hips are square. I keep my chin neutral but my spine tilted at about 35 degrees. My shoulders are hanging slightly out over my toes and my arms are hanging naturally beneath them.

**Figure 8-1-Address Position**
From face on, note that the back of the ball is directly in line with the
left ear at address. My weight is centered between my feet and my
spine is nearly vertical.


## Frame 2 – 9 O'Clock Position

Once my left arm is parallel to the ground, or at about 9
o'clock, we can check to see the shaft is on plane, or
pointing at the inside of the ball. My hands are directly in
front of my right bicep at this point, showing that I am
swinging my arms more around my body rather than up and
down in front of them. This is an ideal position that the
club will travel through during the downswing.

## Figure 8-2 – Halfway Back

Halfway back and the club should be on plane. From face on it is critical that the head and hips remain centered and not slide off the ball away from the target.

## Frame 3 – Top of the Swing

At the top of the swing, the main thing I'm interested in is that the left arm and shoulders are on approximately the same plane so that no complicated rerouting or dropping of the club is necessary from the top of the swing. You can see that I have maintained my spine angle I established at address and the club has the appearance of being slightly laid off at the top, although it is not. If my swing continued on to parallel with this mid-iron, my club would reach parallel to the ground and be pointing at the target. From here, all I want to do is begin unwinding my entire torso back to the left, driving the movement with my core. I like to imagine from the top that I'm throwing a heavy medicine ball down the line to encourage me to use the big muscles of my trunk and core.

### Figure 8-3-Top of the Backswing

At the top of the swing, the first thing we are focused on is getting the weight back to the left side during the transition which happens just before the club reaches the top. If we make a full shoulder turn while remaining centered, we are in a good position to deliver a powerful strike.

## Frame 4 – Downswing Plane

If I've initiated the downswing by just turning everything back to the left while keeping my arms quiet, the club will come right back down the same plane that I took it back on as can be seen in the picture. From this position I can continue to unwind my hips and torso aggressively through the ball while letting my arms and club take a free ride.

**Figure 8-4-Downswing**
If the core of the body initiates the downswing, the arms are carried down perfectly on plane. Note that keeping the arms passive also retains a perfect amount of lag that stores tremendous power while still being easy to control.

## Frame 5 – Impact

Because I was on plane throughout the swing, impact is automatic and a foregone conclusion. This is the benefit of swinging on the 9 o'clock plane throughout the entire swing. It makes your golf swing simple to keep in check and easy to self-check when your swing gets a little off. At impact, you can see that my shaft is on plane and the shaft and my right forearm form a straight line.

**Figure 8-5-Impact**
When the club is on plane at impact and the rotation of the body has
squared the clubface, there is no fear to be aggressive through the

hitting area. My only chore is to "ABT" so as not to "quit" on the shot. If the body keeps turning, I'm assured of a solid and straight shot.

## Frame 6 – Follow Through

Once the downswing begins, the golf swing is running on automatic and there is little that can be done to change the plane that the club is going to come through on the other side of the ball. If the club is released naturally, it should come through parallel to, but above the 9 o'clock plane the club was swung back on.

If your club is not moving through these positions, don't get too worried just yet. There are numerous factors that affect swing plane that are not necessarily bad and can make your swing look very different from this. If you take your arms back deeper earlier in the swing and cock your wrists earlier, you may see a position where the shaft is pointing between your feet and the ball as seen in the following pic:

The important aspect of the Rotary Swing™ plane is that at the 9 o'clock position, the club should NEVER point more than a few inches outside of the ball. This would be indicative of a golfer who takes the club back too deep and shallow early on and excessively rolls his or her forearms during the takeaway or someone who is taking the club back too far to the outside and well above the shaft plane established at address. Ideally it points at a point in between your feet and the ball or directly at the inside of the ball. The danger of being a little "steep" as in the picture above is that it is very easy to get the club "across the line" at the top which tends to lead to an excessively "in to out" swing path. To avoid this, a significant amount of forearm rotation is required to keep the club on plane and therefore, it is not a desirable move.

# Chapter 9 - "Passive" Arms, The Hips & Power

Many golfers get a bit lost when they hear the term "passive" arms because it is a subjective term. Passive to one person might mean something entirely different to another, so let me try and give you some visuals to help you understand exactly what I mean by passive or quiet arms. First, imagine a right-handed basketball player preparing to shot a free throw. Now, imagine the amount of tension in the shooters left arm and hand. There is very little because the right hand is doing all the work, but the left hand is playing an important supporting role. It's not sloppily loose, but "athletically passive". Most importantly, you're not focusing your conscious attention on it; your subconscious is controlling the arm and is far more capable of making necessary last millisecond adjustments if needed for the shot. That is a very important piece of the benefit of passive arms in the golf swing as well. When both arms are athletically passive, the body is in more overall control and the subconscious can and will make subtle corrections as necessary as long as you don't consciously it. As soon as you try and consciously control the club with your arms and hands, you put yourself at risk for an internal conflict between your conscious and subconscious mind and that's not an internal struggle you want. The golf swing is challenging enough without having to wage war with your very powerful subconscious mind.

I have worked with many golfers who like to have their arms very, very soft, almost to the point that they "feel" like they are like cooked spaghetti noodles. I don't think this is necessary, but if you find it works for you, there is no harm in it. Whether they realize it or not, as the swing builds to a crescendo and nears impact, the subconscious will adjust the grip pressure and arm tension to prepare for the strike. This is a natural reaction and one that you have very little control over. Now, imagine the golfer who "death grips" the club right from address. Not only is he going to manipulate the plane and path of the club on the way back, but by the time he reaches impact all his muscles are going to be overly tense and his muscles will be working antagonistically, actually causing him to lose club head speed. Let both of your arms be athletically passive and you will not only increase your distance because soft muscles can move faster than tight muscles, but you will also end up gaining more control of the club by "giving up" what you have felt was control in the past.

If at first you struggle with keeping your arms passive, fear not. I spend perhaps 50% of my teaching time helping the golfer new to the Rotary Swing™ keep his or her arms passive. We use our hands and arms for everything in our daily life. Our hands are very sensitive and provide a great deal of sensory feedback so don't feel bad if you struggle a bit at first. Persevere, it won't take long and know that it has very little to do with technique, it is more of a mental shift of how you think about and feel your golf swing. If you focus your attention on your body and forget about your arms, you will grasp it very quickly. After the first pure shot you hit with passive arms, you will never want to use them in your golf swing again and you will be able to sense immediately when they do become overactive in the swing. It will feel like you have to put a lot more effort into the shot to get the ball to go the same distance and you will notice your shot dispersion pattern will be wider than when your arms are passive.

## What about the Hips?

Much has been written about the role of the hips in the golf swing. While the hips are a very good source of power in the swing, they are a double edged sword. Golfers who have a tendency to drive hard with the legs and hips are in jeopardy of both losing their spine angle and over powering the upper body. A shifting of the hips laterally will tend to drop the club on to a shallower plane during the downswing and can cause the golfer to come more aggressively from the inside. This is not a bad thing as long as the upper body continues to rotate equally aggressively through impact. The problem occurs when the golfer stops rotating, causing the arms to release out away from the body too early in the downswing. At this point, the body is no longer in control of the club and centripetal force will cause the club to work from in to outside the target line. If the clubface is slightly closed to this path, the ball will start right and draw back to the left. If it is square, the ball will be a block, or worse, if the clubface is open, a ball that starts right and goes further right. If nothing else, remember that it's difficult to slide and rotate at the same time. One move will tend to dominate the other and in a Rotary Swing™ you want to remember your "ABT's", Always Be Turning. As long as you continue to turn through the shot with your arms passive, you'll be playing from the middle of the fairway all day.

## Hitting for Extra Power

With all the advances in equipment technology, the game of golf today is becoming much more a power game. You regularly see the big hitters on the professional golf tours driving the ball as far as they can with less and less regard for accuracy. Like it or not, power is an important part of the game and as such, any swing model worth its salt in today's world must be one that has an abundance of power and the Rotary Swing™ does. So, in a Rotary Swing™, how do I find that extra 10 yards when I need it? First, take the advice of the tour professionals who say that when they need extra power, they swing easier. Many people misinterpret this to mean slower, it's not. Swinging easier ensures that everything falls into place in the proper sequence and the muscles stay their softest, allowing them to generate maximum speed and ensure better timing for a solid strike.

Beyond that, allow me to digress a bit into some theory here. For you car buffs, think back to the Wankel rotary engine, most recently popularized by the third generation Mazda RX-7 from the early 1990's. The rotary engine is very different than a typical piston engine found in most cars today and has some interesting characteristics that are applicable to the rotary golf swing. Rather than having a grouping of pistons that move up and down (think "classical" upright golf swing) it has a single piston that rotates in a circle (think rotary golf swing). There is a distinct RPM limit for the up and down motion of the pistons in the classic motor like a V-8 and it is both more complicated and less efficient, but the Wankel has been said to have no theoretical RPM limit. It could theoretically continue to rotate in a circle to ridiculously high speeds (technically, it is not a circle, but an epitroichoid curve, but for the purpose of this discussion, it acts as a good model). The same is theoretically true of the rotary golf swing. When more speed or power is needed, it is gained by speeding up the rotation of the body. Like the Wankel engine, this is simply theoretical for similar reasons to why we would never see a rotary engine operating at 1 million RPMs. There are other dependencies that will limit the speed. For the motor, the spark could only fire so fast and the exhaust and intake valves could not open and close quickly enough to keep up, etc. In the rotary golf swing, the arms still need a little time to drop back down and the hips still need time to clear, etc. However, without going to ridiculous extremes, you can simply speed up your body rotation to get more power out of your swing when needed. Adding power should never be attempted by swinging "harder." An effort to maintain a smooth rotation is always vital, so "swifter" is perfectly acceptable as long as balance is maintained.

# Chapter 10 - Swing Drills, Visualizations & Vocabulary

Apart from the drills mentioned in the context of each section, I also use several other drills to help the golfer with certain tendencies of the swing and to help ingrain the proper sensations and sensory feedback in the swing. Each of these drills is geared around learning the movements of the golf swing, not on learning the position of the golf club.

Because it is difficult to describe these drills in words, a website has been setup at www.RotarySwing.com where you can view over 100 instructional videos online. These videos cover all facets of the game and include dozens of drills specific to the Rotary Swing.

## Drills for the Arms

Learning how to keep the arms passive in the golf swing is as much mental as it is physical, but I do have an excellent drill that will provide the golfer with the proper sensations of keeping the arms passive.

## Broom Drill

Although the Broom Drill gets its name because you use a broom, it can also be performed using a driver with a head cover on it. This makes it a perfect warm up drill that can be done before every round of golf. I will discuss this using a broom because a broom provides the best sensory feedback and can be done at home. Take an athletic erect posture, hold the broom out in front of you with both hands, keep the broom parallel to the ground and pointing at your mid section. Using your body rotation, swing the broom around your body and up on plane with your shoulders, then unwind just as you would when making a normal golf swing while standing erect. Immediately, the resistance of the head of the broom will be felt as you smoothly sweep it around with your body. You will hear a very satisfying "swoosh" sound as you swing the broom. This swoosh sound is very important to developing your rhythm and tempo and you want to hear the swoosh happen as far out in front of you as possible. If you hear it at impact position or before, this means you have released your arms, hands and broom too early and/or stopped rotating. This drill allows your body to feel the resistance created by the broom so that you can feel your body having to work to power the club through impact by rotating. By comparison, you would feel a great deal of effort is necessary to swing it through impact if you actively use the hands. But, by keeping them passive and swinging the broom with the body, you will feel how the smooth rotation of your torso will have no problem sweeping the broom through the impact position. You want this same gradual and effortless feeling of acceleration in your normal golf swing and this is by far the best drill to instill that sensation.

## Head Cover Drill

The head cover drill is very useful at training the left arm to stay connected to, and to be driven by, the rotating torso. If you have a tendency to lift your arms in the swing well above your shoulder plane, this drill will also help break that habit.

Take your normal address position and place a head cover under your left armpit. Make your normal backswing up to the top. At the top of the swing, you should have no trouble keeping the head cover tucked securely under your left arm.

If it falls out at the top, it is obvious that you lifted your arms to arrive at the top of your swing and disconnected your arms from the rotation of your body. If you continue to struggle with this, place another head cover under your right arm and keep it in there throughout the swing. Keeping both upper arms snug to the top of the torso will help you relinquish control of the club to the body and away from the arms and hands. You can hit full shots with this drill, working to keep the head covers in place throughout your swing. The head covers should be allowed to fall out well into the follow through.

## Drills for the Hips

A common tendency in the Rotary Swing™ is for the golfer to slide the hips laterally during the downswing. Note that I call this a tendency and not a fault because it is not. In its simplest form, the Rotary Swing™ is almost purely rotation and this reduces the swing to its fewest moving parts. However, a hip slide can be found in many successful "rotary" type swingers including the great Ben Hogan. In my opinion, for most golfers, a hip slide complicates the movement and introduces more "moving parts", thus increasing the dependency on timing. If you wish to keep the hips quieter but are struggling to do so, I have a drill that will help called the "One Legged Drill".

## One Legged Drill

The One Legged Drill is a very simple drill but is the most important for those who struggle to understand what it feels like rotate properly in the swing, especially with the hips. The drill teaches one of the most important fundamentals of the swing – rotation – while helping to quiet and stabilize the lower body. To begin, take a short iron and place all your weight on your left leg and pull your right foot back behind you. Your right foot is up on its toe for balance only. With the ball off your left foot, swing the club back while keeping your weight completely on your left leg while allowing your hips to rotate on the way back. As you strike the ball your right leg will be pulled out in front of you by the rotation of your body and should end up somewhere near your divot. At all costs, maintain your balance when performing this drill.

If you strike the ball but your right foot stays pulled back behind you it means that you didn't rotate your body through the shot and just swung with your arms and hands. Keep your arms soft and your body turning and you will be able to hit the ball the same distance as you do from your normal address position. This drill helps demonstrate where the power from the Rotary Swing™ really comes from, soft arms and a rotating torso. For bonus points, combine this drill with the Head Cover drill and hit balls with your driver on just your lead leg.

## Visualizations

There are many powerful and useful visualizations and mental techniques that I use when teaching that help instill the proper feelings and motion of the swing. As a matter of fact, many of the fundamentals of the swing are as much a mental exercise than anything else.

## Overactive Hands During the Takeaway

One of the most common tendencies I see in students learning the Rotary Swing™ is for them to get too handsy during the takeaway and abruptly sweep the club too far inside. This will rotate the clubface open, make the swing plane too shallow and deep and put the arms and hands in a position where they must be active during the downswing in order to make solid contact. If you tend to snatch the club away from the ball, imagine that your forearms, hands and the grip of the club are all in a plaster cast for the first part of the swing. This visual will help you take the club back more with the body without any independent arm and hand action. It will help "quiet" down your takeaway making it simpler and more repeatable, and keep you from having to rely on your arms and hands to actively square the clubface at impact.

When the club is halfway back and parallel to the ground, it should be pointing toward the target and be somewhat over the edge of the foot line. The reason to check this "position" is that this is simply where the club naturally moves when you have not manipulated it with the arms and hands and you have correctly rotated your body around your spine. You will also notice that the toe of the club will not be pointing straight up and down as has been customarily taught, rather it will be angled slightly toward the target line in a position that appears to be somewhat "closed". Of course, it is not closed. This is a misnomer in golf terminology and the face is, in fact, actually square to the plane line. It is in the exact same position established at address and has not been manipulated with the hands and arms into an "open" toe up position. If the toe of your club is pointing straight up, you have rolled your left forearm excessively too early in the takeaway and you will be required to roll it the same amount in the opposite direction during the downswing. Rolling the left forearm early in the swing "sets the mood" for the rest of the backswing, if you will, and this rolling will only continue during the backswing. Remember, the more you roll the clubface and forearm during the backswing the more you will be required to roll it back on the downswing. If you go back to the "Passive Arms" section, you will remember there is very little forearm rotation necessary during the backswing and will actually happen completely naturally when your arms are passive.

## Passive Arms

A great visual to help your arms stay passive in the swing is to visualize the Broom Drill during your practice swing. Visualize the swoosh happening more out in front of your body toward the target and "feel" the dragging sensation of the body dragging the arms and broom through impact and beyond.

The best visualization for helping keep the arms passive is actually no visualization at all. Ideally, I'd like for the golfer to completely forget about the arms. Thinking about them turns your focus to them and takes it away from the rotation of the body. In effect, you end up "activating" the arms by "thinking" about them, even if you are trying to think about keeping them passive. Focus on your rotation and the arms will follow.

## Smooooooth

While a golfer can definitely swing the club too slowly, he can never swing it too smoothly. Use all your senses to visualize, hear and feel the club coming through the hitting area smoothly. You don't want to hear an abrupt "whoosh" at the bottom but rather a gradual build up of speed and sound. It will truly feel like you are swinging at half effort, but the speed is there where you need it most. If you've been used to swinging very hard and especially if you swing hard from the top, you will feel like you are swinging at 50% effort. This is because you are used to expending most of your stored energy very early into the downswing. Therefore, you no longer have physics working on your side and actually must swing very hard to get the ball to go anywhere. When the energy in the release of the club is stored by keeping the arms and hands passive, the release happens effortlessly and snaps like a bullwhip at the moment of truth – impact. Therefore, you may not feel as if you are swinging as hard and may not hear the same dramatic "whoosh" you are accustomed to, but trust it and you will be rewarded with the most effortless and powerful golf shots you have ever hit.

## Rotary Swinger's Vocabulary

When I teach a golfer the Rotary Swing, I also start to ingrain a new set of golfing vocabulary words that are often very different than what typically is discussed by other golf instructors. This provides the golfer with new and very powerful mental cues of the proper sensations and feelings he is looking for when the swing is performed properly. Many of the terms or phrases I use overlap and mean the same thing but are simply an attempt to say the same thing a different way in an effort to find something that clicks specifically for the golfer. When you begin to do the drills and the swing correctly, you will quickly gain a fuller and deeper understanding of these terms, but for now, know that these are proper "thoughts" or sensations that are desirable in the swing.

**Effortless** – This is my favorite term. When done correctly, you will be using your big muscles to hit a ball that only weighs 1.6 ounces. Your swing and impact should feel very effortless, to the point that you feel as if you are only putting half as much effort into your swing as before. Strive to develop and recognize this feeling. If you find yourself feeling like you are putting a lot of effort into the swing, realize that the strain you feel is coming from your arms. You don't have near the muscle mass or strength in your arms that you do in your legs, back and core and when you try to use your arms and hands to overpower the shot you will know it immediately.

**Hitting with your body** – Using the big muscles in your body and using them correctly will give you the sensation that you are hitting the ball more with your entire body rather than just your arms or hands. Also, properly rotating your right shoulder back down to the ball will provide you with the sensation of driving your entire right side into the ball. This is a very powerful feeling!

**Quiet** – Because there is very little, if any manipulation of the club face by the arms and hands, the club face will remain very "quiet" throughout the swing – meaning it will not be rolling open a great deal and then rolling shut on the way down. When the clubface stays very quiet throughout the swing this greatly reduces your dependency on timing in the swing.

**I feel more on top of the ball** – This sensation is created directly from doing the "Slide the Shaft" drill correctly as it puts your trailing shoulder more on top of the ball as you come into impact. You will feel as if you are in a very powerful position when you use your entire body to hit **through** the ball instead of hitting **at** it with your arms and hands.

**Half as much effort, but the ball goes further** – This is a very common phrase for the golfer learning the swing. You will literally feel as if you are putting half as much effort into the swing and feel like you're swinging slower because you're not depending on the small muscles of your arms and hands to hit the ball but are employing rotational and centripetal force. If you use your arms and hands as the primary source of power in the swing, it will take more effort and you will feel it immediately. To generate over

100 mph of clubhead speed takes 25-30 pounds of muscle to generate the 4 horsepower necessary to launch the ball with authority. That's a lot of horsepower and you won't find it in the muscles in your arms and hands.

**Turn and Turn** – I know a golfer has "got it" when his swing thoughts are reduced to nothing more than "turn and turn". Simply thinking of turning the body back and turning the body through is the ideal way to view the Rotary Swing and much simpler than the methods instructing you to try to manipulate the club from position to position. When the body is allowed to be the engine of the swing, the only swing thought you need is to "turn and turn."

**Arms felt passive and soft** – A major component to the swing is the arms remaining athletically passive throughout the swing. When done correctly, they feel very soft and feel as if they are following the lead of the body. If you feel like you have a lot of tension in your arms, shoulder and hands, work on letting the club flow around the body with some rhythm and tempo to free up your overall movement.

**My arms did nothing** – A great, but very unique feeling is when you don't really feel your arms do anything in the swing at all. They almost become puppets whose strings are pulled by the body. This is perhaps one of the most challenging aspects of owning the swing, trusting that the arms don't have to do anything active. But the powerful shots you hit when you keep your arms passive will eventually, if not immediately, convince you of this simple truth.

**I felt like I didn't even hit the ball** – Ah, yes, the mysterious shot where the ball that comes off like a missile and you didn't even feel yourself hit it. When you "pure" a golf shot with the Rotary Swing, you will have made a smooth, effortless, body driven swing and the ball will seem completely inconsequential. You won't even feel it get in the way, but you will hear it tear through the air for the first 30 yards. Trust your swing and trust that the smooth rotation of your body will provide all the power you need. Trying to hit the ball hard will only lead to your arms and hands getting overactive and sabotage your efforts to achieve this euphoric feeling.

**Arms felt like they were just along for the ride** – The body drives the swing, the arms, hands and club lag behind and just follow the lead of the body. During the downswing, you want to feel that the arms did nothing active.

**I can't believe the ball went that far** – For many golfers, I really focus in on having them smoothly unwind their bodies at what feels like half speed to them. They are always amazed when the ball goes further than the ones where they feel like they put 80-100% effort into. It only feels slower, but allowing the torso to unwind smoothly actually stores more energy until the very last millisecond of the swing and allows the big muscles to drive the swing, rather than expending it earlier in the downswing before impact. Interestingly enough, the "swoosh" sound is almost imperceptible during the practice and real swings when done at half speed, but the ball goes further because all the speed is released at the very bottom of the swing and is only done so for a split second. This will require trust on the golfer's part because we rely a lot on audio feedback in the golf swing. That is one reason I use the baseball drill where the swoosh happens far out in front of the golfer to help instill this "slow, heavy, relaxed" feeling through impact rather than a "quick, hard, violent" lash that the golfer maybe accustomed to.

**Let's go work on my short game** – When it's all said and done, you realize that learning the golf swing was far simpler than you had been lead to believe. You will realize you don't have to spend nearly as much time on the range banging balls and "working" on your swing. I'm not kidding - I have a lot of people say this to me. It should not take you very long to develop this golf swing. The hardest part will be mentally training yourself to trust it on each swing. The more you work on trusting the effortless power, the easier this will become, but you still need to practice- but a lot more time should be devoted to your short game. A 2:1 ratio for your practice sessions is a good start. In other words, spend twice as much time on your short game as you do hitting full shots. This swing will put you in the mindset that, for the first time, you actually can focus on your short game because you won't have to spend endless hours on the range trying to find or develop some complicated swing made up by "connect the dots". You only need to master a few, very simple fundamentals to hit very good golf shots and once you realize this, your scores, and ball striking will improve dramatically.